THE SISTINE CHAPEL

TEXT BY
FABRIZIO MANCINELLI

EDIZIONI MUSEI VATICANI

Index

English translation by Henry McConnachie

© Copyright 2000
    Ufficio Vendita Pubblicazioni e Riproduzioni
    dei Musei Vaticani
    Città del Vaticano

Photographs: Vatican Museums

Fourth Edition
TIPOGRAFIA VATICANA 2000

The Sistine Chapel

Built in the time of Pope Sixtus IV della Rovere (1471-1484), from whom it takes its name, the Sistine Chapel had originally the functions both of Palatine Chapel and of keep for the complex of buildings set in a square around the Court of the "Pappagallo", the most ancient center of the Apostolic palaces. Later on, as times changed and the Belvedere Courtyard, Borgia Courtyard and Courts of the Sentinel and of St. Damasus came into being, giving a Renaissance character to the papal residence, it lost its defensive function, though the appearance remained, in the severe and massive structure of the exterior and the crenellation of the upper part.

It rises on the site of a "cappella magna" built in the palace by Nicholas III (1277-1280) and used as the popes' chapel until 1477; in that year the thirteenth-century chapel was destroyed or, more probably rebuilt around some of the existing structures.

Today, the building comprises, vertically, a cellar, a mezzanine floor and the chapel, above which lies a spacious attic. The mezzanine floor, like the cellar, is divided into nine rooms, which were the offices of the "Magistri Ceremoniarum". The outside walls rise smoothly, with their bricks visible, their expanse hardly interrupted by the openings that light the interior or by the slightly projecting cornices.

They were crowned by crenellations supported by corbels, with a hole in every two for throwing burning oil and other ammunition on possible attackers.

The chapel is very simple in shape; without an apse, it measures 40.93 meters long by 13.41 meters wide, that is, the dimensions that the Bible gives for the Temple of Solomon. It is 20.70 meters high, and roofed by a flattened barrel vault, with little side vaults over the centered windows. The smoothness of the walls, primed for the painted decoration, is divided, as on the outside of the building, into three cornices, of which the middle and widest one forms a strip running round the perimeter of the chapel at the level of the windows. A low marble seat runs along the walls on three sides in the area reserved for the faithful. The floor is of colored marble inlay, showing how the tradition of the Roman marble workers was still alive in the late fifteenth century, and is divided into contrasting geometrical patterns whose design reflect the architectural distinctions of the chapel (distinguished also by differences in floor level and by the screen). On one side is the presbytery, with the altar and the pope's throne, reserved for officiating clergy, and on the other the space for the faithful. The marble screen with trellises, a free rendering of the Byzantine iconostasis, was moved back during the reign of Gregory XIII to enlarge the presbytery, but originally it was attached to the "cantoria" which, as in Florentine churches, replaces the "schola cantorum". Both are decorated with very delicate reliefs, the work of Mino da Fiesole, possibly assisted by Andrea Bregno and Giovanni Dalmata.

According to Vasari, the architect called to construct the new building was the Florentine Baccio Pontelli, to whom the pope probably entrusted the construction of the Della Rovere palace in Borgo Vecchio. In 1477, however, he could not have been in Rome and in any case the documents mention only Giovannino de' Dolci, who is called "superstans sive commissarius fabrice palacii apostolici". In 1480 the construction must already have been finished, because in 1481 Perugino, Botticelli, Ghirlandaio and Cosimo Rosselli signed a contract to paint ten "stories" in the Sistine Chapel and in the document specific reference is made to frescoes already done.

The arrangement of the chapel, its size and the iconographical programme of the decoration show that the intention of Sixtus IV was to translate into Renaissance terms the composition and structure of the great Paleo-Christian and Medieval basilicas of which there were so many living reminders in Rome.

Pier Matteo d'Amelia, project for the fifteenth century of the ceiling. Florence, Collection of Prints and Drawings, Uffizi

Reconstruction of the Chapel's decoration in the fifteenth century

The Original Decoration of the Chapel

The present decoration of the Sistine Chapel is very different from what was originally planned. The intervention of Michelangelo altered profoundly its severe fifteenth century spatial quality, by bringing into it a whole world of images which overlay its architectural structures, almost replacing them, giving a highly dramatic character to the interior and introducing quite new illusionistic formal elements. When in 1483 the chapel was consecrated, Pier Matteo d'Amelia had painted the ceiling simply as a sky with stars, which centered attention on the decoration below and emphasized the strictly geometrical structure of the vault itself with its horizontal and vertical lines. The original iconographic plan for the decoration included on the wall behind the altar a great frescoed "altar-piece" with the *Assumption of the Virgin* and the two frescoes with the Nativity and the *Finding of Moses* which began the two cycles that continue along the side walls and terminate on the entrance wall. Above began the "gallery" of popes, while on the dado, in accordance with early Christian tradition, were painted simulated curtains. The frescoes on this wall were destroyed to make room for Michelangelo's *Last Judgment,* while the collapse of the architrave over the main door damaged irreparably those on the entrance wall (they were entirely repainted after 1565). Thus, of the original frescoes there remain only those on the side walls.

The decoration of the chapel was done in an incredibly short time, thanks to the close collaboration between the artists and their respective workshops, an example of teamwork rare in the painting of any age. The ambiguity of the documents, of which there are two, dated respectively 26th October 1481 and 17th January 1482, has given rise to contradictory hypotheses as to the chronology of the works. The most reliable, however, seems to be the following. First of all, perhaps in 1480, Perugino was called and decorated the wall behind the altar; later Botticelli, Ghirlandaio and Cosimo Rosselli arrived, and together with Perugino painted on the side wall the first four panels of the Christ cycle, with the curtains below and the corresponding portraits of popes. In October 1481 these four artists promised to carry out by March of the following year the ten remaining frescoes, with the curtains below them, and complete the series of the popes, on pain of forfeiting fifty ducats if they had not finished their work by the date set. Giovannino de' Dolci, of whom we have already spoken in regard to the construction of the chapel, was appointed supervisor of their work, although it is not clear to what extent he performed this task. Payment was to be calculated on the basis of the decoration already done on the side wall, which in January 1482 was estimated at two hundred and fifty gold ducats.

The four artists, helped by the workshops —which counted among their members Pinturicchio, Piero di Cosimo and Bartolomeo della Gatta—painted at the same time the scenes of the two cycles, Christ and Moses, and advanced parallel, as was the custom, toward the entrance wall. There must have been a preliminary agreement, as all the figures are uniform in size and the horizon line is at the same height in all the frescoes, the homogeneity of the whole, transcending the stylistic differences between the artists, has suggested that one particular artist may have been responsible for directing the others; Vasari

(continuation, see p. 8)

5

Plan of the Sistine Chapel
with list of paintings

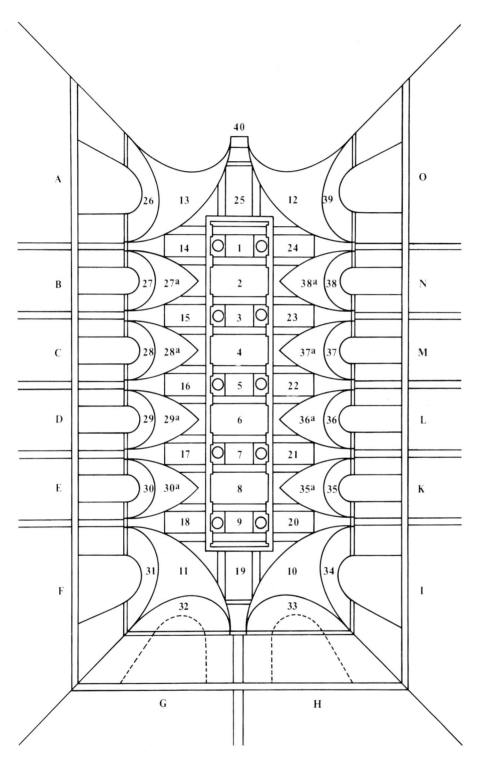

A Perugino and Pinturicchio
   Mose's Journey into Egypt
B Sandro Botticelli
   Scenes from the Life of
   Moses
C Cosimo Rosselli
   Crossing of the Red Sea
D Cosimo Rosselli assisted by
   Piero di Cosimo
   Moses and the Tables of the
   Law
E Sandro Botticelli
   Punishment of Korah, Datan
   and Abiram
F Luca Signorelli
   Testament and Death of
   Moses
G Matteo da Lecce
   Fight over the Body of Moses
H Van den Broeck
   Resurrection of Christ
I Cosimo Rosselli
   Last Supper
K Perugino
   Handing Over of the Keys
L Cosimo Rosselli and
   Piero di Cosimo
   Sermon on the Mount and
   Healing of the Leper
M Domenico Ghirlandaio
   Calling of the First
   Apostles
N Sandro Botticelli
   Temptations of Christ and
   Purification of the Leper
O Perugino and Pinturicchio
   Baptism of Christ

MICHELANGELO
 1. Separation of Light and
    Darkness
 2. The Creation of the
    Sun and Moon
 3. The Separation of Land and
    Water
 4. The Creation of Adam
 5. The Creation of Eve
 6. The Fall and Expulsion from
    Paradise
 7. The Sacrifice of Noah
 8. The Flood
 9. The Drunkenness of Noah
10. Judith and Holofernes
11. David and Goliath
12. The Brazen Serpent
13. The Punishment of Haman
14. Jeremiah
15. The Persian Sibyl
16. Ezechiel
17. The Erythrean Sibyl
18. Joel
19. Zechariah
20. The Delphian Sibyl
21. Isaiah
22. The Cumaean Sibyl
23. Daniel
24. The Libyan Sibyl
25. Jonas
26. "Aminadab"
27. "Salmon, Booz, Obeth"
28. "Roboam, Abias"
29. "Ozias, Ioatham, Achaz"
30. "Zorobabel, Abiud,
    Eliachim"
31. "Achim, Eliud"
32. "Iacob, Ioseph"
33. "Eleazar, Mathan"
34. "Azor, Sadoch"
35. "Iosias, Ieconias,
    Salathiel"
36. "Ezechias, Manasses, Amon"
37. "Asa, Iosafat, Ioram"
38. "Iesse, David, Salomon"
39. "Naason"
40. Last Judgment

⇨
View of the Chapel, towards the Last Judgment

Perugino and Pinturicchio, Mose's Journey into Egypt, detail

maintains that Sixtus IV called Botticelli from Florence for this purpose, but it is more probable, if the theory is in fact true, that the role fell to Perugino; he was highly esteemed by his colleagues and since he was the first to begin the pattern of his works conditioned that of the others. It was he who painted the greatest number of scenes—besides those on the altar wall, he painted the *Baptism of Christ,* the *Handing over of the Keys to St. Peter* and the *Circumcision of the Son of Moses.* As for the others, Botticelli painted three panels, Ghirlandaio two and Cosimo Rosselli four. There has been some controversy over the attribution of the single scenes, but the account of Vasari, which is supported by stylistic indications, is generally accepted. The question of the portraits of the popes is more debatable,

but in view of the terms of the contract it is probable that each artist was responsible for those above the scenes he himself painted. For reasons unknown to us, the decoration of the apel was not finished by the artists that began it, and in Autumn 1482 Luca Signorelli was commissioned to paint two missing frescoes, the *Testament of Moses* and the *Fight over the Body of Moses.* The next year the Chapel was completed, and on 15th August Sixtus IV della Rovere performed the solemn consecration, dedicating it to the Virgin of the Assumption (perhaps the name also of the thirtheenth-century church).

The *Stories of Moses* originally began with the description of the early childhood of the prophet, and among the episodes in the lost fresco, according to Vasari, were the *Birth and*

Sandro Botticelli, Scenes from the Life of Moses, detail

the Finding of Moses. The biblical account now begins with the *Journey of Moses;* in this panel, against a hilly background we see in the fore the meeting of the Prophet and the Angel, sent by the Lord to punish him for his disobedience to the order to circumcise all his male children, and on the right the circumcision of his son. The title *Observatio antiquae regenerationis a Moise per circoncisionem* refers to this last episode, and in both scenes the figure of Zipporah, who becomes the main protagonist and who personifies the Church of the Gentiles, is given great importance. In the background we see Moses taking leave of

Sandro Botticelli, Scenes from the Life of Moses, detail

9

this father-in-law Jethro, before setting out on the journey back to Egypt during which he meets the Angel. The fresco is generally attributed to Perugino, who however was to an important extent assisted by Pinturicchio, probably the painter of the delicate landscape.

The second panel is the work of Botticelli, and illustrates as many as seven events from the life of Moses. The story begins, below right, with the killing of the Egyptian who had maltreated a Jew (right) and the consequent flight into the desert (above). In the center is the meeting with the daughters of Jethro, whom Moses helps to water their flocks after chasing off (in the background) the shepherds who were trying to stop them. The most important episode, as regards iconographical content, is, however, that of the burning bush (above left) to which the title accompanying the painting refers (*Temptatio Moisi legis scriptae latoris*). This is a clear allusion to the test to which Yahweh subjected the prophet, ordering him to walk into the burning bush after taking off his shoes. The story finishes below with Israel leaving Egypt, led by Moses, who has become the guide and leader of his people.

The third panel, rather weak in composition, is generally attributed to Cosimo Rosselli and Piero di Cosimo, although it has also been suggested that it is by Ghirlandaio, who painted the *Calling of the First Apostles* opposite. It shows the *Crossing of the Red Sea,* and this single episode, in contrast to the previous frescoes, takes up almost all the available space; the group of little figures in the background on the right probably represents Moses and Aaron before Pharaoh, who is granting them permission to leave Egypt.

The title *Congregatio populi a Moise scrip-* *tam accepturi* refers to the episode where the people are gathering joyfully around the figure of the Prophet (below left), for the first time singled out by the composition. Beyond the historical meaning, which can clearly be read in the scene, the inscription highlights a symbolic content, the expectation of the Law, and stresses the fact that this scene is a prelude to the next in which the "promulgatio" of the Law takes place—the *Handing over of the Tables of the Law*. This painting is also by Cosimo Rosselli, and it is both the most archaic and the weakest by the Florentine master. It seems that he had won the liking of the Pope who, as Vasari recounts, "did not understand much about these things, although he took great delight in them". This fresco, besides the Handing over the Tables of the Law (center above), comprises the Adoration of the Golden Calf (center background), Moses breaking the Tables of the Law (center foreground), the Punishment of the Idolaters (right above) and the return of Moses with the new Tables of the Law (left), to which more specifically the title *Promulgatio legis scriptae a Moise* refers. With this series of episodes the role of the prophet changes; from now on he is represented as a Law-giver, and thus mediator between the Jews and God. Beside him Joshua is constantly seen, while the figure of Aaron is given slight importance.

The fifth panel, the most important of the series from the point of view of symbolic content, was painted by Botticelli, who presented a subject iconographically very rare, the *Punishment of Korah, Datan and Abiron*. In contrast to the previous ones, the episodes are set in a landscape which we could call urban, dominated by three classical buildings of which

(continuation, see p. 12)

Cosimo Rosselli, Crossing of the Red Sea, detail

Cosimo Rosselli and Piero di Cosimo, Handing over of the Tables of the Law, detail

Sandro Botticelli, Punishment of Korach, Datan and Abiron

two are clearly recognizable, the Septizonium on the right and in the center the Arch of Constantine, the writing on which admonishes *Nemo sibi assum / at honorem nisi / vocatus a Deo / tamquam Aaron.* The action occurs in the foreground: on the right the attempt to stone Moses, referred to in the title (*Conturbatio Moisi legis scriptae latoris*); in the center, at a sign from Moses, the followers of Korah who were offering incense are consumed by an invisible fire, contrasting with Aaron, a hieratic priestly figure with a tiara; to the left, again at a sign from Moses, the earth opens up to swallow the blasphemers, while their children watch the scene in terror as if suspended on a cloud.

The last fresco on this wall is devoted to the *Testament of Moses* and was painted by Luca Signorelli; lost, as we have already said, is the *Fight over the Body of Moses,* which concluded the series and was also by Signorelli. The present painting was entirely redone at the time of Gregory XIII by Matteo da Lecce, a mediocre Mannerist. The *Testament of Moses* is divided into five episodes set in a hilly landscape not very different in composition from that in the first fresco. The title *Replicatio legis scriptae a Moise* refers to the episode in the right foreground, showing the prophet as he reads the law; in the center is the nude figure of the foreigner, and on the left Moses hands over the rod of command to Joshua. These two episodes stress the last aspect of the character of Moses, his priestly quality. In the background the angel shows Moses Jerusalem from the top of Mt. Horeb, while below he descends toward the place of his death, represented in the episode on the left.

(continuation, see p. 14)

⇨
Sandro Botticelli, Punishment of Korach, Datan and Abiron, detail

The *Stories of Christ* are also without the first scene representing the *Nativity,* which was destroyed to make place for Michelangelo's *Last Judgment.* The story now begins with the *Baptism of Christ,* the work of Perugino, whose signature can be seen on the band above the scene. The Umbrian master was, however, largely assisted by Pinturicchio, who probably painted most of the figures, excepting the central group, and the delicate landscape in the background. The Baptism which occupies the center foreground of the panel is referred to in the title, *Institutio novae regenerationis a Christo in Baptismo,* which stresses the correspondence of this painting with the one opposite, thus leading the spectator to a parallel reading of the scenes, which is then extended to all the frescoes on the walls. In the right background is Christ preaching, and on the left a sermon of John the Baptist.

The second fresco, the work of Botticelli, is devoted to the *Temptations of Christ,* which strangely, although they are the main subject of the picture—the title *Temptatio Iesu Christi latoris evangelicae legis* seems to refer to them—are represented in three successive episodes in the background. In the foreground is depicted a sacrificial rite which some have interpreted as the Purification of the Leper, while others see in it a symbolic content which transcends the "historical" significance of the scene—the priest is supposed to be Moses, representative of the old law by which the offering of blood is made, and the young acolyte is supposed to be Christ, the bearer of evangelic law, destined to redeem humanity by the sacrifice of his own blood.

The following painting, the only one remaining by Ghirlandaio, represents the *Calling of the First Apostles,* and is divided into a series of three scenes, of which the two in the background depict respectively the Calling of Peter and Andrew and the Calling of James and John. In the foreground are Christ and the kneeling figures of Andrew and Peter; the latter is made to stand out, as also in the *Handing over of the Keys,* as if to emphasize his role as Christ's successor. The Redeemer, who is obviously represented as the leader of the people "congregated" under the new law, dominates the center of the picture, as does Moses in the fresco opposite. The correspondence of meanings uniting the two paintings is stressed by the title, *Congregatio popoli legem evangelicam accepturi.*

There follows the *Sermon on the Mount* in which Christ takes on the character of legislator, as is stressed by the title *Promulgatio evangelicae legis per Christum.* The old law, delivered by Yahweh to Moses on Mt. Sinai, is thus contrasted with the law of the Beatitudes given by the Redeemer in his sermon. To the side is depicted the miracle of the Healing of the Leper. The fresco is swarming with figures, the work of Cosimo Rosselli, but the splendid landscape, cut across by a duck in flight, was painted, as Vasari records, by Piero di Cosimo.

The fifth panel, the most important of the series for its symbolic content, represents the *Handing over of the Keys* and is considered the masterpiece of Perugino, although some see the hand of Signorelli in some of the figures of Apostles. The scene, like the one opposite of the *Punishment of Korah,* is set in a city landscape—a great square, dominated by a domed building to the sides of which are symmetrically placed two triumphal arches, faithful copies of the Arch of Constantine. In the background we note the Payment of the

Luca Signorelli, Testament and Death of Moses, detail

Tribute Money and the attempted Stoning of Christ, referred to in the title *Conturbatio Iesu Christi legislatoris,* which once again stresses the Redeemer's role as law-giver. The two figures to the right in the foreground, one with a setsquare and the other with a sextant, are Giovannino de' Dolci and, perhaps, Baccio Pontelli; facing them is a figure with a thick mane of dark hair around his face, thought to be Perugino's selfportrait.

The last fresco on this wall, the *Last Supper,* was again painted by Cosimo Rosselli with the help of Piero di Cosimo. The composition is quite traditional, with the exception of the addition of the still life and the two animals in the foreground. In the background are the Agony in the Garden, the Capture of

Christ and the Crucifixion. The title *Replicatio legis evangelicae a Christo* refers to the main episode in which Christ, as in the corresponding scene of the Stories of Moses, assumes the role of priest as well as that of legislator, concluding the sequence of meanings that unifies the two cycles of frescoes.

Lost, as we have already said, is the masterpiece by Ghirlandaio depicting the *Resurrection of Christ,* repainted at the end of the sixteenth century by the Dutch painter Arrigo Fiammingo (Van der Broeck). There remains today only the title, although faded and incomplete, *Resurrectio et ascensio Christi evangelicae legis latoris.*

An iconographic program like that of the Sistine Chapel could certainly not have been

Perugino and Pinturicchio, Baptism of Christ, detail

left to the free will of the painters called to carry it out. It presents, in fact, many layers of meanings, which go from the traditional illustration of events from the Old and New Testament, to the pairing of episodes from each cycle on the basis of their typological similarity. Moses is in fact the best known precursor of Christ, and the necessity for exemplifying this theme, also in the titles, conditions the choice of episodes for both cycles. But alongside these meanings, which must have been obvious to the contemporaries of Sixtus IV, there is an evident intention to communicate another message, which becomes clear only on a careful reading of the two sets of stories. Moses is presented successively as leader, legislator and priest, and the same qualities are illustrated in the figure of

Christ; of these aspects the titles stress especially the power to establish law. Now, these qualities were handed down to Peter as the founder of the papacy in the fresco of the *Handing over of the Keys,* which is itself the key to the interpretation of the whole wall decoration. It is no chance that in the background is shown the Payment of the Tribute Money, which alludes to the superiority of spiritual power over temporal, and the Arch of Constantine recurs twice—Constantine was the emperor who according to tradition officially sanctioned this power by his donation. To this we must add that the fresco opposite, the *Punishment of Korah,* contains a severe warning to all those who, even from within the church, try to throw doubt on the

(continuation, see p. 20)

16

*Sandro Botticelli, Temptations of Christ
and Purification of the Leper*

*Sandro Botticelli, Temptation of Christ
and Purification of the Leper, detail*

Domenico Ghirlandaio, Calling of the First Apostles

Cosimo Rosselli and Piero di Cosimo, Sermon on the Mount and Healing of the Leper

Perugino, Handing over of the Keys

Perugino, Handing over of the Keys, detail

Cosimo Rosselli, Last Supper

authority of the papacy—a warning which becomes even more evident if we take into account the inscription painted on the triumphal arch, which once more reproduces that of Constantine. Similar concepts to those expressed in the stories in the Sistine Chapel—often, like the text of the inscription, drawn from the letter of St. Paul to the Hebrews—recur often in the writings of Sixtus IV, who at that time was fighting the threat of the Council of Basel which, manoeuvered by kings and bishops, aimed at weakening the powers of the papacy. This background explains also the presence of the gallery of "portraits" of the first thirty popes, which originally began with the images of Christ and Peter; it has the function, like the stories below, of documenting the historical origins of papal power.

This programme is also the basis for the choice of a structural (in the sense of organization of interior space) and decorative pattern for the chapel based on the ancient proto-Christian basilicas, such as St. Paul's and St. Peter's, which had witnessed the foundation of the Church's temporal power. Significantly, however, the Pope did not confine himself to a mere return to ancient times, but called some of the most "modern" artists of his own day to give his message a contemporary form.

The content of this message was not altered by his successors; with the tapestries of Raphael (now in the Vatican Pinacoteca) and the frescoes of the ceiling and altar wall by Michelangelo it only became richer and more far reaching.

The Ceiling

The popes who succeeded Sixtus IV limited themselves to completing some details of the work which had remained unfinished. As is indicated by the fragments which have recently come to light in the Sacristy, Innocent VIII covered the cross vault of this room with a painted wooden surface and affixed his own coat of arms on it in polychrome marble; Alexander VI carried out the fresco decoration of the walls, which is now lost, with the exception of some fragments and the painted coat of arms which miraculously survived in one of the lunettes. Alexander's also is the marble coat of arms which appears in the chapel on the lintel of the door to the right of the altar. Subsidence problems began to affect the Sistine Chapel right from the start of Julius II's pontificate, perhaps as the result of the excavations carried out both to the north and to the south of the building, at the foot of the hill on which the Apostolic Palace stood, to create the foundations of the Borgia Tower and of the new St. Peter's. In May 1504 a long diagonal crack opened on the chapel ceiling, causing such damage that it was closed for about six months.

Bramante tried to remedy these structural problems, bringing into use the chains that are still visible today in the great ceiling above the vault, but the damage suffered by the fresco decoration was so serious that it convinced Julius II to plan its complete resurfacing and to entrust the project to Michelangelo.

The decision to embark on the project coincided with the exact moment of the artist's dispute with the pope and his flight to Florence: dated the 10th of May 1506 is in fact the well-known letter of Piero Rosselli in which he informed Michelangelo, who was in Florence, of the talks between himself, the pope and Bramante and of the doubts raised by the latter as regards his ability to realise such a complex project as the decoration of the Sistine Chapel. In substance Bramante affirmed that Michelangelo "only wished to do the tomb (of Julius II) and not the painting (of the chapel)" which faithfully echoed the artist's wishes, and added "I believe he doesn't have the heart for it because he has not done too many figures and most of the figures are high up and are foreshortened and this is another thing from painting on the ground".

If the presumed and apparent maliciousness of some of Bramante's declarations was such as to unleash the anger of the fiery Rosselli, it must nevertheless be pointed out that the doubts raised by the architect from Urbi-'no were not in fact groundless, given that as far as fresco painting is concerned, apart from his probable participation in a subordinate capacity in the decoration of the Tornabuoni Chapel in S. Maria Novella in Florence (1488), it does not appear that Buonarroti had previously produced anything more than the Cartoon for the Battle of Cascina, that is only one work which moreover remained at the drafting stage.

The problems mentioned by Bramante were therefore apparently real and it is surprising that Michelangelo succeeded in overcoming them as if they were inexistent, giving us with the decoration of the Sistine Chapel an extremely complex product from the point of view of perspective construction and at the same time—as the recent restoration demonstrated—of a qualitative level which, on the technical level, makes it the painted equiva-

(continuation, see p. 26)

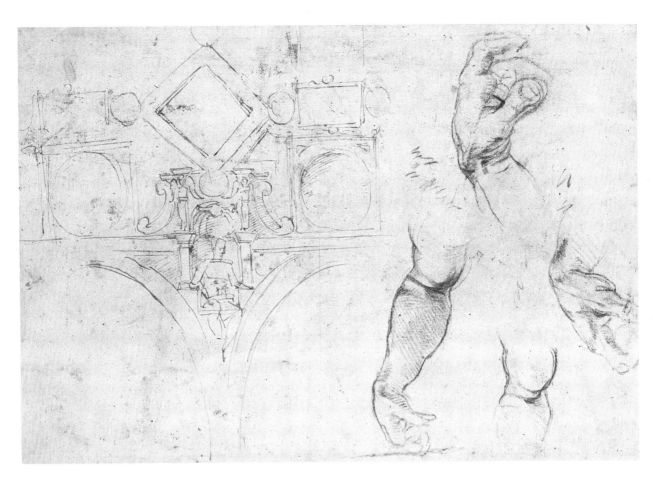

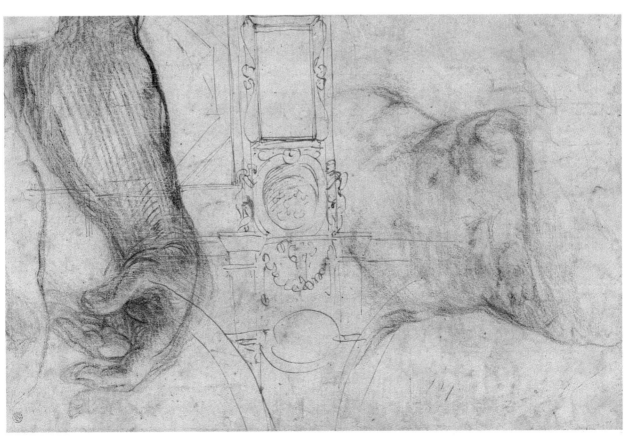

⇨
*Figure study
for the ceiling
frescoes.
London,
British Museum*

⇦
*Study
for the decoration
of the ceiling.
London,
British Museum*

⇦
*Study
for the decoration
of the ceiling.
Detroit,
Institute of Arts*

lent of a treatise or painting in *buon fresco*.

At the end of bitter resistance which lasted for well on two years, Michelangelo had to bow to the pope's will and on the 8th of May —curiously the same day as Rosselli's letter—he signed the contract, agreeing, on the estimate of Giuliano da Sangallo, on a lump sum which he subsequently complained about on several occasions—for example in the 1523 letter to Battucci—because it evidently turned out to be much less than was due.

The initial iconographic programme was very simple and consisted of the twelve Apostles in the pendentives—even if in the 1523 letter "lunecte" were erroneously mentioned and for the "rest a certain portion full of adornments as is used". Soon afterwards —according to the same letter—on the entreaty of Buonarroti, to whom "it seemed it would not turn out well", the Pope gave him a "new commission that I should do what I wanted".

And so Michelangelo created above the last cornice of the Chapel an imposing mock architectural structure composed of five arches open in the centre and interspersed by four rectangular spaces: in effect a monumental arrangement open in imagination to the outside, beyond which there appear in the form of visions nine stories from Genesis —six episodes of the Creation, from the *Separation of Light and Darkness* to the *Expulsion*, and three scenes from the life of Noah, that is the *Sacrifice*, the *Flood* and the *Drunkenness*—intended to illustrate the origins of man, his fall, his first reconciliation with God and the promise of future redemption. At the sides of the spaces situated in the centre of the arches ten wingless angels depicted as *Ignudi* are seated on stone plinths supporting what Vasari describes as "medals, within which are stories in rough sketch, simulated in bronze and gold taken from the Book of Kings". Finally, at the base of the structure, corresponding to the arches, are twelve monumental thrones upon which are seated the figures of the Seers, that is to say the Sibyls and the Prophets, who in a more or less clear manner foretold the coming of the Redeemer to mankind.

Depicted in the lunettes and their overhanging spandrels (below the images of the prophets and sibyls) are Christ's ancestors, while in the four corner spandrels appear the biblical heroes and heroines—Judith, David, Moses and Esther—who by their deeds—the *Beheading of Holofernes,* the *Slaying of Goliath,* the *Bronze Serpent* and the *Punishment of Aman*—bear witness to the existence of a divine plan of salvation for the chosen people.

The series of the Ancestors typologically corresponds to the place at the beginning of St. Matthew's Gospel which starts from Abraham and not from Adam, as in St. Luke's text. This is a relatively unusual theme without many figurative precedents, which Michelangelo developed creating a surprising gallery of individual characters, subtly investigated from the psychological viewpoint and seen particularly in their being united in family groups, with a series of portrayals of the subject of the mother with her children, which are among the most novel and effective images of the entire decorative cycle.

The reason why the series of the Ancestors was included in the iconographic programme of the Sistine Chapel is not completely clear: from the thematic point of view Christ's forebears form part of the representation of the tree of Jesse, in which the Prophets and Sibyls reappear, but beyond this and other possible reasons, it cannot be excluded that among the determining elements there could have been the fact that on the occasion of some feasts of the Blessed Virgin—at least from 1507 onwards—the "Liber Generationis Iesu Christi" of Josquin des Prez, a motet dedicated to the genealogy of Jesus derived from St. Matthew's text, was rendered in the Chapel.

⇦
The Sistine ceiling

Detail of the Sistine ceiling

There is no real structural connection between the world of the Seers and that of the Ancestors: in fact the illusionary plan of the ceiling does not rest materially on that below the lunettes and the spandrels, but is simply juxtaposed in an extremely free relationship, dialectic in type. An apparent connection, not real but imaginary, is created by the presence of bucranes, objects full of meaning perhaps alluding to the fleetingness of life, at the side of which the *Bronze Nudes* are arranged.

Most probably the latter are portrayals of the *Rebel Angels* and constitute the earthly pendant of the *Ignudi:* their nature is revealed on the one hand by the colour of their bodies and on the other by the gesture with which the couple above the spandrel of Jesse point to their ears which are clearly luciferine as are the fingers with their long claws.

On many occasions in the past scholars emphasised the neo-platonic nature of the Sistine Chapel's iconographic programme, while more recently there has been the hypothesis of a relationship with Savonarola's preaching. According to the letter sent to Fattucci it was Michelangelo himself who was responsible for the programme, but the witness of the artist has been placed in doubt many times by criticism which, for the most part, has preferred not even to speculate about a relationship of collaboration with the learned theologians of the papal court.

The most articulated suggestions have come primarily from Frederick Hartt who hypothesised that the originator of the schema was the Franciscan Marco Vigerio, author of the "Decachordum Christianum", published in 1507 and dedicated to Julius II from whom the theologian received his red hat. Of a different opinion is Esther Gordon Dotson who, contrary to Hartt, maintains that the cycle does not depend on the teachings of St. Bonaventure but on those of St. Augustine and that the schema was drawn up by Egidio da Viterbo, one of the most authoritative theologians of the Della Rovere court, who was Vicar General of the Order and—thanks to the studies conducted in Florence with Marsilio Ficino—fully informed on neo-platonic theories.

The hypothesis that Michelangelo effectively had a predominant role in the drafting besides the realisation of the iconographic programme was recently advanced by Charles Hope. It is however without doubt that at the moment of depicting individual motifs Michelangelo often introduced variations, even re-elaborating or reinventing them, as in particular in the case of the series of the Ancestors which radically differs from any pre-existing example.

Although the idea of renewing the decoration dates back to the spring of 1506, Michelangelo did not make any studies for it before the signing of the contract two years later. Both the London and Detroit studies still linked to the project of the twelve Apostles are in fact after that date, particularly the elaboration of the definitive scheme that Michelangelo could not however have been able to determine in its individual details without having the work scaffolding available; the ceiling of the Sistine Chapel is in fact a policentric and moreover a so-called "Roman ceiling"—with then an extremely irregular surface—on which precise measurements could not have been made from the ground. The first problem that the artist had to tackle was therefore that of the scaffolding: the Sistine was in fact the pontifical chapel and differently from the time when Sixtus had it restructured and decorated, had to remain usable throughout the whole period of the work, as a result of which it was necessary to devise a structure that would in no way obstruct the lower part.

Initially the task was entrusted to Bramante who planned and perhaps constructed a suspended platform supported by ropes which, according to Vasari and Condivi "perforated the ceiling"; a very similar structure to the one used afterwards by Pietro da Cortona to fresco the ceiling of the Salone in the Palazzo Barberini. This solution was not to Michelangelo's liking probably both because of its lack of stability and because it raised the problem of how to fill in the holes through which the ropes passed. He asked Bramante's opinion and then came the reply—"We shall think about it later"—which did not please him, so he asked the pope and obtained permission to do what he wanted.

The structure built by Michelangelo was also pensile and substantially consisted of the adaptation into scaffolding of a framework to prime the ceiling. It had a central platform from which the artist depicted the episodes from Genesis and the Ignudi; with lateral steps from which he painted the series of the Seers and the spandrels; while from another platform,which ran at the base of the scaffolding and to which access could be gained by removing the boards of the steps, he frescoed the Ancestors in the lunettes. In essence this was an erection which enabled work to be done on any part of the ceiling, without obstructing the space below where the customary liturgical ceremonies could be—as in fact they were—celebrated.

A picture of this structure seen in section has been preserved for us by a very lively

(continuation, see p. 30)

Separation of Light from Darkness

Creation of the Sun and Moon

sketch in pen on the border of a drawing which is now in the Uffizi: Michelangelo probably drew it when the bridge was re-mounted in 1511 to show the bridge-builder how the work should be carried out and he did so using the first sheet of paper he had at hand, significantly a study for the *Creation of Man,* that is the first scene executed with the second bridge.

The bridge was constructed by Piero Ros-selli to whom Buonarroti had also entrusted the task of chiselling out the pre-existing decoration and applying the layer of plaster so that it would have time to dry out perfectly during the summer months: despite this the novelty of the Roman materials pozzolana (volcanic dust), travertine lime—also created problems with the arrival of winter, so much so that Giuliano da Sangallo had to intervene to resolve them. In July of 1508 these operations were completed and the immediately subsequent period was used to go ahead with the graphic projection of the frescoes—certainly commenced already by May and to identify and purchase the necessary colours.

During this phase the artist was probably assisted by Aristotele da Sangallo who had experience in the construction of scaffolding and possessed remarkable knowledge of per-spective, qualities in both cases coming from his family upbringing and his association with Bramante: also with him was Francesco Granacci, a childhood friend whom Michelangelo appointed to select the "garzoni" (apprentices) to be employed and who was given the job of foreman with the task, among others, of helping him in his search for colours.

In October all the preliminary operations had probably been completed and it seems that it was at this point that Buonarotti summoned to Rome the assistants chosen for him by Granacci. Thanks to different sources and Michelangelo's papers we know the names of all the members of the team: besides the aforementioned Granacci and Aristotele there were Giuliano Bugiardini, Angnolo di Donnino and Iacopo di Sandro. There were differences with the latter—perhaps of a financial nature—right from the start and in January Iacopo left Rome and was quickly replaced by Indaco Vecchio, that is by Jacopo di Lazzaro di Pietro Torni, who like most of the others came from Ghirlandaio's workshop and had therefore that type of training which enabled him to fill, in an appropriate manner, the position that had remained vacant. To these were added Giovanni Michi, a man of whom we know little besides his name, who

Creation of the Sun and Moon

was given the job of handyman. According to the sources the members of the workshop were employed in the Sistine Chapel for a very short time and Michelangelo "seeing what they had done was far from approaching his expectations or fulfilling his purpose, one morning he determined to destroy the whole of it" (Vasari).

In reality things turned out differently: the assistants remained on the scaffolding for about a year and what they did was not limited to auxiliary supporting tasks, like the execution of the ornamental parts of the cornice. Their presence can be seen clearly in the putti in the reliefs of the Seers' thrones and in the monochrome tondi and also, though less obviously, in the three stories of Noah, the first realised by Buonarotti who started to work from the area opposite the entrance wall leaving to the last that above the altar.

This is a recognisable presence particularly because of a qualitative falling-off of the images and the adoption of operational techniques different from the point of view of the

(continuation, see p. 33)

⇨
Creation of the Sun and Moon,
detail of the Creator

Separation of Land and Water

thickness of the colour, of the methods used in preparation, of the finishing touches, etc. This can be seen in the group of the Children of Noah, in the *Drunkenness,* in some parts of the *Flood* and in the *Sacrifice,* in figures such as that of Noah's wife, which denotes a sort of executive timidity—in the way of applying the brush-strokes and in the use of an outline understood as a limit—none of which could be attributed to Michelangelo who in the same space of time had painted figures like the *Delphic Sibyl,* the *Ignudi* around the *Drunkenness* or, in the *Flood,* the figure of the old man disembarking on the islet bearing the body of his dead son.

The presence of the assistants does not nevertheless mean that they enjoyed the customary relative freedom of Ghirlandaio's workshop: in fact Michelangelo exercised very rigorous control over the assistants with every probability that he intervened personally in finishing the work of some of them which explains the generally very high qualitative level, despite local, limited falling-off in tone. Be-

sides this probable direct intervention, the main instrument of the control exercised over the assistants was the preliminary execution of very accurate cartoons for almost all the figures on the ceiling, basically with the one exception of the Ancestors in the lunettes, of the Bronze Nudes at the side of the spandrels and probably of the shield-bearing putti. This must have involved the use of a remarkable quantity of paper, a material which at the time was decidedly costly and it is tragic to note that not even one example of that incredible graphic treasure has survived; of "4 pieces of the cartoons of the Chapel, of the Ignudi and the Prophets" we know that at the time of Vasari they were in the possession of the heirs of Girolamo degli Albizi; the one of the *Drunkenness* was given as a gift to Bindo Altoviti and as for the others, according to Michelangelo's papers, it seems that many were burned in 1517 following his own instructions.

Of the cartoons only traces remain today

(continuation, see p. 38)

Creation of Adam, detail

⇦
Creation of Adam

Creation of Adam, detail

of the systems that were used to transpose the design, but thanks to these elements we know with certainty for what figures they were used; we also know that while for the first half of the ceiling the outline of the images was transposed with a fine dusting of powder—with the one exception of the figure of the decapitated Holofernes and of the Angel of the *Expulsion* —in the second half there was a distinct change in method as a result of which the dusting powder continued to be used for the figures of the Seers and of the Ignudi and in part for the corner spandrels, while in the scenes from Genesis—excluding the *Creation of Man* where both techniques appear—and in the spandrels above the lunettes engraving was constantly used: a method that could be carried out very quickly in which much was left to the inventiveness of the moment the paint was applied. The sketching of the cartoons was preceded by very accurate graphic projection: this is borne out by the number and characteristics of the drawings which have come down to us including a series of very quick compositional and analytical sketches, generally of small dimensions and for the most part contained in the so-called Oxford Notebook, followed by ever more precise studies of the figures and of individual details on larger sheets, generally in charcoal or in red chalk, but also in pen, although this is much rarer and, it appears, limited to the first third of the ceiling.

In this planning stage, differently from Raphael for example, Michelangelo does not appear to have used the workshop and in all probability he did not use it either for the sketching of those drawings on the plaster—of whose existence we have many indications which he used to study *in situ* the composite plan on the one hand and on the other the individual figures or groups: these obviously preceded the sketching of the cartoons and were of fundamental importance for those parts that were executed without using them, such as the lunettes.

The realisation of the painted architectural structures which act as a frame for the biblical scenes and as a prop for the figures of the Seers, of the Ignudi and of the Ancestors must have been particularly exacting. Both the master and the assistants were certainly involved and given the extreme irregularity of the surfaces the draft design must have been continually adapted to the local situation. As it was carried out directly *in situ* engraving the plaster with a scalpel and making use of nails, cords and a ruler the imprint of the modifications made on the original tracing remained impressed on the mortar and give evidence of the attention with which Michelangelo followed the completion of the plan in every single detail, pre-arranging among other things some cartoons for the repetitive ornamental parts—acorns and shells—of the cornices of the spandrels. Although the artist had summoned expert assistants, all coming from the best Florentine workshops, his lack of practice with the materials—lime and pozzolana— which were used in Rome for plasters, initially created the problems described by the sources: they were resolved with the assistance of Sangallo but the damage done obliged Michelangelo to re-do the *Flood* which—as the sequence of the work that could be done in a day indicates—was certainly the first fresco completed on the ceiling.

Of the initial version the master kept only the group of fugitives on the island and as the work continued he refined his operational technique of all those solutions partially *a secco* that he had adopted in the previous drafting, painting almost exclusively in *buon fresco* with the exception of some second thoughts and for the tondi where the presence of gilding obliged him to work differently. Dealing moreover with a ceiling, he adopted a type of drafting without body, often very like watercolour, constructing the images with a dense web of brush-strokes, at times thicker and close in order to create a marble-like and translucent surface, at times left more sparse so as to make the background more transparent: the result is a very luminous painting, made to be legible in all weathers and therefore in every light, of an almost maniacal per-

Creation of Eve

fection without harming the feeling of extreme freedom that is disclosed by every single detail. Having overcome the initial difficulties the work proceeded quickly towards the altar wall, continuing with every probability from the top to the bottom and span by span: in the same way broadly speaking so too must the drafting have proceeded and it is not probably by chance that when studies of more than one figure appear on one sheet they always refer to the same span.

As the scaffolding allowed this the lunettes too were executed within the framework of the same campaign: perhaps all together at the end of each piece of scaffolding or perhaps proceeding step by step with the work on the ceiling above. The apparent differences and especially the greater expressive freedom that they denote with respect to the figures of the ceiling are not in fact due to reasons of a chronological nature, as De Tolnay maintained, but to the absence of a preparatory cartoon: drawn and painted with extreme ra-

(continuation, see p. 42)

⇨
The Original Sin and Expulsion from Eden

The Fall, detail of Eve

pidity and with an enormous average of almost four square metres to be painted in a day, the lunettes are in reality great gouaches, that is large coloured drawings with expressive freedom of drawing and subsequently with greater modernity than the more refined images of the ceiling.

In all probability in September 1509 Michelangelo changed the composition of the workshop, doing without the support of some of its members—in particular Granacci and Bugiardini, the former subsequently becoming active in Florence—perhaps replacing them from then on with others who were less prestigious, more precisely with Giovanni Trignoli and Bernardino Zacchetti from Reggio. The departure of the assistants must have coincided with the realisation of the scene of the *Original Sin:* here in fact the compositional plan changes radically, becoming reduced to a few figures whose proportions increase remarkably reaching a height of more

The Expulsion from Eden, detail of Eve

Ignudo

Sacrifice of Noah

Ignudo

than two metres, and here the rhythm of work extends the areas to be completed in a day's work and a subsequent decrease in their number: for example in the scene of the *Expulsion* the figure of Eve is two metres high and was completed in only one work session. In essence, with the *Original Sin* conditions were created which made the intervention of the workshop in the Stories inappropriate and forced Michelangelo to limit its use to the secondary parts—tondi, reliefs on the thrones—and to the decorative scheme.

In August 1510 the artist had "done half, that is from the door to the middle of the ceiling" (Condivi), but at the beginning of September he had to interrupt the operation because of the Pope's departure which left him "with no orders, in such a way that I am with-

(continuation, see p. 48)

⇨
The flood

The flood, detail

⇦

The flood, detail

Judith and Holofernes

out any money, nor do I know what I have to do". The "half" completed by Michelangelo went "from the door" that is to to say, from Zachariah to the *Creation of Eve* and laterally included the Seers to the *Cumaean Sibyl* —curiously *Ezechiel* was instead realised with the second scaffolding—and the lunettes as far as Roboam and Asah: essentially limiting himself to the area above the presbytery. Here in effect,the system of transposing the design of the cartoon to the ceiling and for the lunettes, the plan of the areas to be completed in a day's work which no longer includes the fascia that acts as a cornice to the windows, changes radically.

The Pope's absence obliged Michelangelo not to proceed for about a year and only on the occasion of the feast of the Assumption in

1511 was the scaffolding dismantled and the artist was able to show Julius II what he had done: the pope gave his assent to continue and on the 1st of October he gave him an advance of 400 ducats. According to Hirst it is likely that it was around this time that work started again on the scaffolding which in the meantime had been re-erected on the second half of the chapel.

What followed was an incredible "tour de force" which was completed scarcely a year later, in October 1512, allowing Michelangelo to write finally to his father: "I have finished the chapel that I was painting: the pope is very well satisfied".

"I felt in discovering it the whole world rushing from every part and this was enough to make people remain astounded and dumb-

(continuation, see p. 50)

Judith and Holofernes, detail

David and Goliath

struck", this was how Vasari described the effect produced by the unveiling of Michelangelo's masterpiece. In reality right from the first dismantling of the scaffolding in 1511, the work was approved of and won the enthusiastic admiration of everyone and first among these was "Raphael from Urbino, who was very excellent in imitation, having seen it immediately and suddenly, to show his virtue, changed his manner and did the Prophets and the Sibyls of the Work of Peace" (Vasari). However, going beyond the frescoes of S. Maria della Pace recalled by the biographer from Arezzo, the most direct "comparison", because it was carried out in the Vatican, Raphael compared it with the decoration of the ceiling of the Stanza di Eliodoro, which in the scene of the *Disembarkation from the Ark* contains textual references to the *Creation of Man* and to the spandrel of *Judith,* just as the extremely watercolour-like application of the paint is clearly derived from that of the Sistine ceiling.

In his own circles Raphael was obviously not the only one to fall under the spell of Michelangelo's masterpiece and Giulio Romano too, when he had to fresco the *Fall of the Titans* in the ducal palace in Mantua, bore

The Brazen Serpent

it in mind, creating a composition which contains very clear references to the spandrel of the *Brazen Serpent*.

Stylistically the ceiling is a product that is still typically Florentine, both from the formal point of view, as the restoration demonstrated, as well as the chromatic. The taste for essentially cold colour is in fact Florentine, veined with intellectualism and basically not naturalistic, and Florentine too is the techno-figurative culture that permeates the images: at its origin there is on the one hand the experience lived in Ghirlandaio's workshop and on the other the memory of formal solutions in the manner of Filippino Lippi that are par-

(continuation, see p. 63)

Prophet Jeremiah, detail

⇨
Persian Sibyl

⇦
Prophet Jeremiah

⇨ ⇨
Prophet Ezekiel

Prophet Joel

⇦
Erythrean Sibyl

Prophet Zecchariah, detail

⟵
Prophet Zecchariah

Delphian Sibyl

⇨
Prophet Isaiah

Cumaean Sibyl, detail

⇨
*Putti painted in false relief
on the throne of the Cumaean Sibyl*

ticularly obvious in the *Ignudi* above the *Prophet Joel*.

The four years it took to complete the undertaking were not however without their effects on Michelangelo and the process of becoming more mature can already be seen in the passage from the *Ignudi* surrounding the *Drunkenness* to those of the subsequent spans which denote less severe surroundings and softer and more gradated modelling: a still more clear-cut and radical departure from the original culture can then be noted in the images realised with the second scaffolding

(continuation, see p. 73)

⇦
Cumaean Sibyl

Lybian Sibyl

⬅

View of the vault with the "Separation of Light from Darkness", "Creation of the Sun and Moon", "The Libyan Sibyl", and the cove with "The Parents of the Future King Jesse"

Prophet Daniel, detail

⇦
Prophet Daniel

IONAS

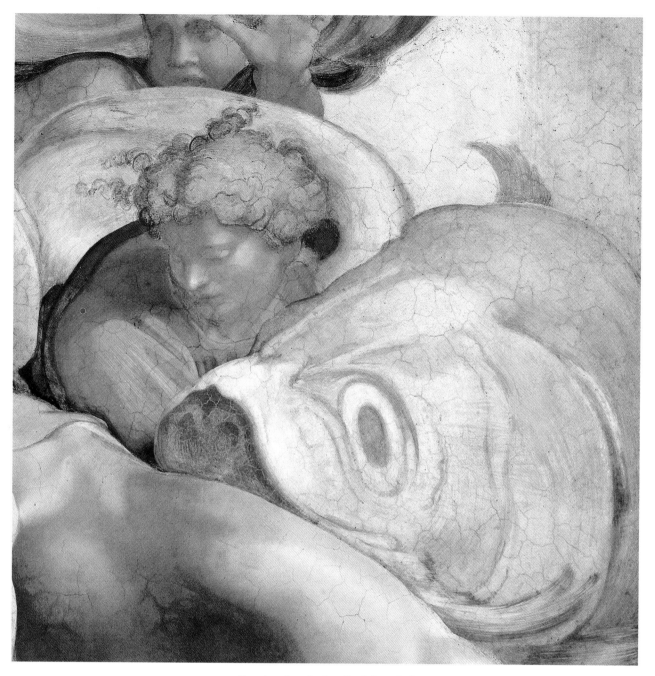

Prophet Jonah, detail of the whale

⇦
Prophet Jonah

⇨
Partial view of the vault

EZE

Ignudo

Ignudo

which display more than anything else greater monumentality in the planning. This different monumentality, the boldness of the perspective solutions undertaken, the extremely acidulous colours and the very frequent use of changeant, could obviously not but have had extremely early effects on those who were to become the putative sons of Michelangelo, from Andrea del Sarto to Rosso, Pontormo and to Domenico Beccafumi.

⇨
Ignudi and medaillon with Jehu destroying the image of Baal

Cove with the family of Zorobabel

Cove with the child Roboam and his mother Abia

Cove with the family of Ozias

Cove with the child Solomon and his mother

Lunette with Achim and Eliud

Lunette with Ezekias, Manasses and Amon

⇦
Lunette with Jacob and Joseph

The Last Judgement

After the ceiling which Julius II managed to see completed shortly before his death (21st February 1513), the Chapel was further embellished under Leo X, a Medici, who in 1515 or shortly before, commissioned Raphael to do the cartoons for a series of tapestries with the Stories of the Apostles Peter and Paul. The cartoons—seven of which are now in the Victoria and Albert Museum in London—were completed between June 1515 and October 1516: the tapestries—at present in the Vatican Picture Gallery—were woven in Peter van Aelst's workshop in Brussels and displayed for the first time in the Sistine Chapel on the 26th of December 1519, arousing the admiration of all who were present, who, according to the Master of Ceremonies, Paris de Grassis, judged them "superior in beauty to anything else on earth".

Michelangelo's second involvement in the decoration of the Chapel is due to another Medici: if in fact it was Paul III, a Farnese, to finalise the project, the commission for Michelangelo to do the *Last Judgement* was the result of the choice and the wishes of Clement VII.

It is generally maintained that Clement and Michelangelo discussed the project right from the time they had a meeting in Florence on the 22nd of September 1533 and according to Vasari the pope asked the artist "that on the main (facade) where the altar is, he should paint the Last Judgement so that he could show in the story everything that the art of drawing could achieve: and that on the opposite wall, above the main door, he ordered him to do so to show when because of his pride Lucifer was expelled from heaven and cast down into the centre of hell with all those Angels who sinned with him".

A much more complex project therefore than the one that had been effectively realised and which perhaps had its distant roots in the time of Julius II. On the death of Pope Clement, Michelangelo who had wanted to return to devote himself to the tormented project of the "Tomb" of Julius II, tried to get out of this or at least to postpone the Sistine project and faced with Paul III's insistence reminded him of the agreements he had already established with the Duke of Urbino. It seems that Paul III then became agitated and exclaimed: "I have wanted this for thirty years and now that I am Pope will you not satisfy me? I shall tear up the contract and I am prepared for you to serve me in every way" (Vasari).

Faced with the Pope's wishes, just as before at the time of Julius II, Michelangelo had to give in to Paul III "wanting him to continue the cartoon ordered from him by Clement, without altering anything in the invention or concept that had been given to him" (Vasari). It is not likely that already at the time of Clement there were many "cartoons and drawings" ready as one could be led to believe from another passage from Vasari, but the drafting must have started in the spring of 1534 and before the death of the Pope on the 25th of September that same year and that the artist could have shown Leo X what Condivi called "cartoons", that is apparently a "model" on a reduced scale of the composition. From this phase there remain two studies, one in Bayonne in the Musee Bonnat and the other in the Uffizi in Florence, the first relating to Christ the Judge alone and to surrounding figures, the second to the overall scene. The Uffizi drawing is of particular in-

(continuation, see p. 82)

⇨

Last Judgement

terest because it seems to indicate that initially Michelangelo wished to preserve both the two lunettes, of which there is no trace on the Florentine sheet, as well as the altar-piece of the Assumption, whose cornice is instead clearly traced out in the base at the centre, flanked by the resurrected and by the damned who are cast down into hell.

The composition already presents many elements of its final appearance and particularly denotes the dynamic attitude which differentiates Michelangelo's *Judgement* from any other example painted previously: clearly outlined in the drawing are the "attitudes" of Christ and of the Virgin and therefore the nature of the complex psychological relationship which unites the two personages is defined: but both the Redeemer's gesture and the pose of the Virgin have a violence and an excitement that will be greatly toned down in the fresco, interiorising more than being explicit about the emotive elements of the subject.

To bind the artist definitively to his wishes Paul III, with two Briefs of September 1st, 1535, nominated him "supremum Architectum Sculptorem et Pictorem eiusdem Palatii nostri Apostolici... ac nostrum Familiarem cum omnibus et singulis gratiis prerogativis honoribus oneribus et antelationibus quibus alii nostri familiares utuntur et uti possunt seu consueverunt", granting him a life stipend of one thousand two hundred scudi a year—a truly remarkable sum—of which six hundred came from the toll of the Passo del Po near Piacenza and the same again from the Dataria, with payment generally made every two months or more. In the Briefs it is specified that the stipend was granted "pro depingendo a te pariete altaris Capellae nostrae pictura et Historia ultimi Iudicii,... et ceteris operibus in Palatio nostro a te si opus fuerit faciendis".

If therefore Clement had truly planned —as the sources indicate—to have Michelangelo paint both the *Fall of the Rebel Angels* and the *Last Judgement,* Paul III limited the task to the latter theme, preserving its unusual positioning on the altar wall planned by the Medici Pope. This was one of Clement VII's choices not inspired by improbable artistic reasons, as suggested by the sources, but carried out to effect a warning of what the Sack of Rome signified for the Church and to express his own anguish and dismay "when faced with events that seemed to destroy every certainty at its roots" (De Vecchi): a gesture not without "symbolic significance that probably went far beyond the pontiff's understanding and intentions" (De Vecchi), but to which his successor subscribed in full.

Work started on the 16th of April 1535 with the construction of the scaffolding, followed by a period of several months which was partly used to demolish the pre-existing decoration—Perugino's frescoes and the two lunettes dating from the time of Julius II but also in part was occupied by disputes which, as Vasari recounts, led to the breaking of relations with Sebastiano del Piombo. Sebastiano had in fact persuaded the "Pope that he should have Michelangelo do (the 'facade') in oils, whereas he only wanted to do it in fresco. As Michelangelo said neither yes nor no and, arranging the facade in the manner of Brother Sebastiano, Michelangelo did not lift a finger for several months; but then being asked he finally said that he wanted to do it only in fresco and that painting in oils was merely for women, the rich and the slothful, like Brother Sebastiano; and so he tore down the encrustation done on the friar's orders and had everything plastered over so that he could work in fresco, and then Michelangelo set to work" (Vasari).

The Venetian's "plasterwork" was demolished on the 25th of January 1536; on the following 13th of February there was the payment for the "bricks... to line the wall" that Michelangelo wanted to incline forward, more exactly "that it should jut out from the top by about half a 'braccio'—the actual projection is 24 cm.—so that no dust or other dirt could settle on it" (Vasari). Finally starting on the 18th of May they began to purchase the paints and in particular the very costly "ultramarine"—or rather lapis lazuli—that Buonarroti used without any compunction for the great surface of the ceiling, also because all the expenses were covered by the Commissioner of the Pontifical Fabric, Iacopo Meleghino. The true and proper work of painting must have started between the end of spring and the beginning of summer that year and proceeded from the top towards the bottom, probably starting from the lunette on the left, the one with the Cross and the Crown of Thorns supported and borne in flight by wingless angels.

After the realisation of the second lunette there was probably a pause in the drafting of the areas to be completed in a working day, as would seem to be suggested by the marked unevenness between the surfaces of the lunettes and the areas below; what the reasons were is not clear, but it is possible that the time was spent in preparing the cartoons of the fascia with Christ, the Virgin and the Elect.

A cartoon was undoubtedly prepared for all the figures in the Judgement with the exception of only a few images—generally in the second row—which were realised *a secco* at the time of the drafting on the plaster: none of them has survived but here and there traces remain of the methods used in transposing the drawing, less visible than on the ceiling because the paint always has a certain body and is rarely in watercolours. In all probability these preparatory drawings were made gradually as the work proceeded and curiously, like on the ceiling, in the lower part of the composition, that is to say in the final phase of the work, the dusting powder alternates with the engraving, mostly confined to the figures of the demons.

From a technical point of view, the Judgement is painted in *buon fresco* just as Michelangelo said he wished to do in order to spite Sebastiano, however there are very many exceptions to the rule.

First of all in the choice of paints as regards the earthcolour and the oxides—such as lapis lazuli—pigments appear that adapt poorly to the technique of fresco or even colours—like lacquer, giallolino and orpi-

ment—which can only be used *a secco*. Constantly, moreover, the many changes are *a secco* and these are generally determined for visual reasons, just like the additions of figures in the background made directly *in situ* to increase the sense of depth of the composition.

All this bears witness to the metamorphosis undergone by Michelangelo from the time of the ceiling, his detachment from the technical and formal solutions of the Florentine world, of which he was a creature, and his interest in a chromatic taste on which on the one hand there must have weighed his intimacy with Sebastiano del Piombo and on the other his stay, albeit brief, in Venice, where he had taken shelter in 1529. In saying this we do not mean that in the Judgement Michelangelo adopted a Venetian method of painting, but undoubtedly the warm light of the scene all played on the dominant ultramarine blue of the sky in a very obvious manner and shows signs of the feeling of the light and colour of Titian and of great Venetian painting of the time.

On the 15th of December 1540 the work must have been well advanced because the scaffolding was lowered and the upper part of the painting uncovered, perhaps in order to control from ground level the correctness of the foreshortening; a problem which at the time of the ceiling was posed essentially only for the last span.

Towards the end of the undertaking there was also an accident: Michelangelo fell from the scaffolding and hurt his leg, but initially "in the pain and the anger (sic) this caused him" he refused medical attention. Tended by force by his surgeon friend Baccio Rontini he recovered quickly and "having returned to his work, he laboured continually for some months when he brought it to an end, giving so much force to the figures that they verified the description of Dante: 'Dead are the dead, the living seem to live'; the sufferings of the damned and the joys of the blessed are exhibited with equal truth" (Vasari).

(continuation, see p. 85)

Study for the Last Judgment, detail. Florence, Collection of Prints and Drawings, Uffizi

Detail of St Bartholomew and the flayed skin showing the features of Michelangelo

By the end of October 1541, on All Saints Day, the same day on which the ceiling saw the light for the first time, the Judgement was also unveiled, giving rise to very great scandal and admiration. Like all the "stories" in the Sistine Chapel, the Judgement too was conceived as a vision taking place beyond the space of the chapel: there are no architectural compartments of any kind and it is as if the wall suddenly disappeared and beyond it the scene of the last day appears.

It takes place in a space that denotes the very nature of the aforesaid and this analogy is brought out by the fact that on the right the Cyrene (or good thief, whoever he may be), who obviously belongs to the space of the representation, seems to rest the Cross on the cornice below the pontiffs, that is on an element which forms part of the surroundings for worship. The crowd of the elect and of the damned, like those of the risen, visibly comes from outside the scene and their being outwith the real architectural structure is indica-

(continuation, see p. 87)

ted and emphasised at the same time by the positioning of the figures at the edges of the representational space and by the emergence alongside the Cyrene of the hands of a person who is evidently situated beyond the wall.

The composition is conceived as an architectural complex of bodies, arranged, although with many variations according to the traditional hierarchical order, but articulated on different planes, in depth, and engaged in a slow and relentless elliptical movement by the imperious but at the same time calm gesture of Christ the Judge. He is depicted at the centre, in the act of rising from His throne of clouds, with the serene and inscrutable countenance of the Omniscient, His arms raised as if to call for attention and at

the same time to calm the surrounding turmoil. Beside Him the Virgin turns her head in a gesture of compassion, her body twisted round in a movement that contrasts that of Christ, almost as if to emphasise the diversity of their roles: she however no longer intercedes as on the Uffizi sheet but limits herself to awaiting the result of the judgement with trepidation.

Above, in the lunettes, two groups of wingless angels bear in flight the instruments of the Passion; on the left the Cross, the dice and the crown of thorns; on the right the pillar of the Scourging, the ladder and the staff with the sponge soaked in vinegar.

Around Christ and the Virgin the Saints and the Elect slowly form a circle in expectation. Significantly their movements and attitudes do not display happiness or relief, as could be expected, but anxiety and concern: the moment represented is in fact contrary to all tradition, that immediately prior to the pronouncement of the verdict.

Last Judgement, detail of angels with symbols of Christ's passion

Among these personages from left to right one can recognise Adam, his shoulders covered with an animal skin—the sources identify him instead as St. John the Baptist—St. Andrew with his cross, St. Lawrence with the gridiron, the flayed St. Bartholomew holding his own skin, St. Peter with the keys and alongside him perhaps the Baptist: at their feet Dismas, the Good Thief, with his cross, St. Simon the Zealot with a saw, St. Blaise with the combs used for carding wool, St. Catherine of Alexandria with a broken spiked wheel, St. Sebastian on bended knee with arrows in his hand and behind him the Cyrene, the Cross bearer. Above to the right the old man with the tangled beard must be Moses and on the extreme left the old woman with blind eyes who is removing the veil from her face reminds one of the Cumaean Sibyl of the ceiling.

In the fascia below, at the centre there is the group of the trumpet-blowing angels, with to the left the risen ascending into heaven and below the resurrected some of whom are la-

Last Judgement, detail of trumpeting angels with the book of Good Deeds (left) and book of Evil Deeds (right)

boriously emerging from the earth, others again as skeletons without flesh. To the right angels and demons compete in casting the damned down into hell, while below, with clear reference to Dante's text which was well known to Michelangelo, Charon with the blows of his oar and the demons armed with grappling-irons make the damned disembark from a boat which restoration has revealed was winged and covered with feathers, to bring them to their judge Minos, depicted below to the right, his body locked in the coils of a serpent, indicating the turnings to which each one is destined.

The contemporary identifiable characters, all of whom are connected with Michelangelo in a very direct way are few: the young Elect depicted on the extreme left could be Cavalieri almost at the same level as St. Blaise— dressed in red with his hair prematurely white; according to some St. Peter could have the features of Paul III and St. Bartholomew those of Pietro Aretino, while a self portrait of the artist is normally identified in the skin of the saint; the closeness of the figure with the receding temples behind St. Bartholomew could suggest identifying him as Urbino, that is the assistant who actively collaborated with the master and to whom with all probability the rare qualitative shortcomings of the fresco are due.

The presence of the portrait of Pietro Aretino in the Judgement could have been determined, at least in part, by Michelangelo's wish to soften the blow of refusing the offer made to him on the 15th of September 1537 of a compositional plan for the fresco; the artist justified his refusal by the fact that "having completed a great part of the story, I cannot put your imagination into work".

The homage, admitting that it can be considered such (given that Michelangelo ironically inserted his own portrait in the skin of the flayed man) did not have the desired effect and in 1545 Aretino was among his most violent critics as can be seen from the text of the letter he sent to him in November of that same year where among other things he asked him: "Well then, that Michelangelo so stupendous in fame, that Michelangelo so notable in

prudence, that Michelangelo so admired, did he wish to show people no less irreverence and lack of religion than perfection in painting?" Aretino's criticism was not an isolated phenomenon and motions of censure were expressed right from the time the work was in course, in particular by the Master of Ceremonies Biagio da Cesena who having climbed up the scaffolding with the Pope "was asked what he thought of the performance. To this he replied that it was a very improper thing to paint so many nude forms, all showing their nakedness in that shameless fashion, in so highly honoured a place; adding that such pictures were better suited to a bath-house, or a road-side wine-shop, than to the chapel of a Pope. Displeased by these remarks Michelangelo resolved to be avenged; and Messer Biagio had no sooner departed than our artist drew his portrait from memory without requiring a further sitting, and placed him in hell under the figure of Minos, with a great serpent wound round his limbs, and standing in the midst of a troop of devils: nor did the entreaties of Messer Biagio to the Pope and Michelangelo that this portrait might be removed suffice to prevail on the master to consent; it was left as depicted, a memorial of that event, and may still be seen" (Vasari).

The polemics, as is borne out by this episode and the previously quoted letter from Aretino, were very violent right from the time of Paul III, but the greatest danger came with Paul IV who planned to destroy Michelangelo's masterpiece to enlarge the chapel towards the sacristy. Previously Paul IV, a Carafa, had asked the artist to "mend" the fresco and that he sarcastically replied: "Tell His Holiness that this is a mere trifle and can easily be done; let him mend the world, paintings are easily mended".

The official decision to "mend" the Judgement was taken by the Congregation of the

(continuation, see p. 95)

⇨

Last Judgement, detail of the resurrection of the dead

Detail of the elect on the left

⇦
Detail of the resurrection of the dead

⇨
Detail of the elect with John the Baptist

Detail of the elect, St. Peter

Council of Trent at the time of Pius V which on the 21st of January 1564 decreed: "Picturae in capella Apostolica coperiantur, in aliis autem ecclesiis deleantur, si quae aliquid obscoenum aut evidenter falsum ostendant".

It is to be noted that the decree was not directed exclusively at the Judgement but was of a more general nature. In the Sistine the task of painting the first covering drapes, the

⇦
Detail of the elect on the right of Christ.
Below are Saints with the instruments of their martyrdom

so-called "braghe" or breeches, was entrusted to Daniele da Volterra who in 1565 re-did the figure of St. Blaise in fresco modifying his attitude and still in fresco re-clothed the figure of St. Catherine, while Adam's and certainly the Cyrene's "breeches" were painted *a secco*.

As is shown by Venusti's copy Daniele's "breeches" were only the first of a long series: even in the 18th century in fact, Richard noted that in 1762 he had seen "very mediocre artists engaged in covering the most beautiful nudes of the painting and of the ceiling with draperies".

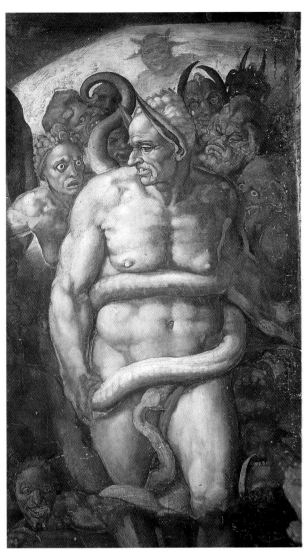

Last Judgement, during the restoration; Minos, judge of the underworld, with the semblance of Biagio da Cesena the Chamberlain who critized Michelangelo's work

⇨ *Last Judgement, Charon with the oar brings the condemned to the Inferno.*

The restorations between 1964 and 1993

The restoration of Michelangelo's frescoes on the ceiling—which brought to light the brilliant typically Tuscan colour scheme, hidden up to now by deteriorated layers of restoring size and other extraneous substances—is the natural continuation of the work done between 1964 and 1974 on the frescoes with the *Episodes from the Lives of Moses and of Christ* on the side walls of the chapel.

At the end of that first work cycle, significantly begun on the occasion of the centenary of Michelangelo's death, attention moved to the conservation problems of the building itself which, while not having shown any defects on the structural plane for centuries, had also had roofing problems in recent times, as often in the past. And so, in 1975, on the centenary of Buonarroti's birth, it was decided to carry out the restoration of the roof, of the great apartment below—originally intended as quarters for the guard and of the sentry passage behind the Guelph battlements, which were restored to their original form removing the plugs which broke the rhythm. Obviously the metal trusses of the roof installed under Leo XIII and which by this time had become a relic of industrial archaeology were preserved. In the guard-room a very light steel platform was erected halfway up, to make it possible to reach the small windows for regulating their opening, ventilating the area and for carrying out eventual maintenance work on the roof without walking on the extrados of the ceiling: a grid was attached to the window frame which, when the windows were opened, would prevent the possible entry of birds or bats and the resulting deposit of guano. The grilled level of the platform allowed for a working overload of 150 kgs per sq.m., more than sufficient for the purpose for which it was intended, but such as to discourage its use for any other purpose. A problem for which a solution was sought at more or less the same period was that of the mock draperies below the Lives of Christ and Moses. Work was first started in 1964 on that below the panel with the *Testament of Moses* and this brought out the extent of the repainting and the very poor state of preservation, especially in the lower part, but did not clarify exactly what the decoration was meant to represent: mock tapestries as in common parlance, mocked stamped leather or something else. The cleaning begun in 1975 on both the north and south walls showed that in fact they were mock damasks, while the work on those of the entrance wall revealed that this area had been completely redone on the occasion of the operation datable to the reigns of Pius IV and Gregory XIII radically altering the representation of the mock materials and creating great curtains of a uniform brown hue, apparently without any ornamental features. The documentary research conducted recently by Anna Maria De Strobel and Edith Cicerchia revealed that the transformation of the mock damasks of Sixtus IV—"brocaded" to quote Taja's words—into mock tapestries, was done at the time of Pope Clement XI (Albani), who had this fascia of fifteenth century decoration entirely repainted *a secco* by Filippo Germisoni.

In 1979 the restoration of the Mosaic and Christological cycle was resumed, to be completed with the cleaning of the two scenes of the entrance wall seriously damaged by sixteenth century despoilers of the chapel and entirely redone, between the pontificates of Pius IV and Gregory XIII, by Matteo da Lecce and Hendrick van den Broeck.

(continuation, see p. 100)

Punishment of Haman

The cleaning of the two large panels completed in July 1980 drew attention to the existence of a problem of the level of cleaning: the decision wisely taken in 1964 on the Lives of the side walls to reduce only partially the layer of dirt and extraneous substances (glues, grease, dust and soot) could not in fact be maintained in this case because of the different techno-conservation situation. On the Matteo da Lecce, the removal of the superficial restoration retouchings and a first coat of extraneous substances left an extremely broken surface, stained, with a general greying and blurring of tones: the oldest repaintings moreover, that is to say those which probably in the eighteenth century had radically altered some details, remained in place.

On the scene by Hendrick van den Broeck —which had finishing touches *a secco* on a fresco base and consequently much damaged by earlier cleanings—the removal of the very extensive retouchings of restoration and that, only partial, of the glues and greases of similar origin, caused an identical result of greying and blurring of the images.

This made more extensive cleaning essential even if the decision left open the possibility of having to intervene in the future to the same extent also on the already restored panels of the fifteenth century frescoes of the side walls.

In the spring of 1980 when the restoration of the *Resurrection of Christ,* and of the *Fight over Moses' Body* was nearing its conclusion, the scaffolding to make a start on the cleaning of the Pontiffs was erected. One section of the scaffolding was set up directly in front of the *Eleazar-Mathan* lunette for the purpose of carrying out a precise series of observations and exploratory tests, in order to have the largest possible amount of data available at the moment of the operation, planned at the conclusion of the restoration of the *Pontiffs.* However, examination of the lunette disclosed the presence of very minute cracks in the colour fabric, to be found above all over the entire ceiling. Laboratory tests showed that what was responsible for the damage was the glue which covered these like all the other frescoes of the chapel: as a result of changes of temperature and humidity it tended in fact to shrink and to curl up into very small scales, causing the aforementioned cracks. Laboratory tests and *in situ* observations also proved beyond any shadow of doubt that the applying of the glue was the result of old restoration, the main purpose of which was to revive the colour of the frescoes severely darkened by the dust and soot of the candles and oil lamps used to light the chapel. In specific coloured areas greatly enlarged, between glue and paint, there appeared a layer of dust and soot which evidently had taken at least many decades to deposit itself on the painted surface; besides this the glue concealed the presence of extensive salification caused by the infiltration of rain-water and the related damage. Since by its very nature the phenomenon of the cracks was destined to continue, intervention on Michelangelo's decoration could no longer be delayed. Following a long chain of research and experiments a cleaning method was adopted which involved the use of the so-called AB57, a solvent mixture prepared for some time by the Central Institute of Restoration and widely used. AB57 is composed of ammonium bicarbonate, sodium bicarbonate, Desogen (an anti-fungicide) and carbossilmeticellulosa and it acts instantly. In the case of the ceiling frescoes the mixture was allowed to remain on the area to be cleaned for about three minutes and then removed together with the extraneous substances—swollen and softened by it—by means of a damp natural sponge, sterilised and soaked in twice-distilled water: in cases where it was seen to be necessary the treatment was repeated after 24 hours. The *a secco* parts—very few and limited to some second thoughts, besides the gilding and the drawing of the monochrome medallions—being sensitive to water were cleaned last with specific organic solvents or with those methods which permitted the use of watery solvents after having been fixed in advance with a solution of Paraloid B72 dissolved in nitrate thinner.

Last Judgement, detail of the elect on the left, during the restoration

The first cleaning trial was carried out in June 1980 on the figure of Eleazar in the lunette of that name and the results were examined by the commission in charge of the restoration which decided to extend the work to the entire surface. The restoration of the lunette was completed on the 10th February 1981 and the results were presented to the public, the press and scholars. The authoritativeness and number of favourable opinions strengthened the decision to extend the work to Michelangelo's other frescoes in the chapel, for which a plan was worked out which envisaged the cleaning of the fourteen lunettes together with the 28 *Pontiffs* below (finished in 1984), then the ceiling (finished in 1989) and finally the *Judgement,* completed in 1994.

The operation consisted almost exclusively in the cleaning of the frescoed surfaces, in that the consolidation of the plaster had already been carried out in the time of Seitz and Biagetti, and the level of cleaning was determined by the complete recovery of all the subtle chromatic passages foreseen by Michelangelo without which the image would turn out to be flat and bereft of modelling; on the painted surface however there was left that very light

(continuation, see p. 105)

The Creation of Man, detail of the touching fingers during the cleaning.
Visible on Adam's finger tips are the reparations by Domenico Carnevale, after the damage to the vault

The Original Sin,
detail of the tempter serpent during the various phases of the cleaning

⇨ *Putto holding a plaque,*
detail during the cleaning.
Dark stains are visible
along the cracks of the plaster
and the fading of the colors
caused by water infiltration

⇦
The Creation of Man, detail of the touching fingers
during the cleaning; on the left, still not cleaned,
is visible the restoration of Carnevale on the darkened
lesion which crosses the figure vertically

veil of dirt which formed and settled on the fresco, partly contemporaneously with the carbonisation of the plaster, in the first years of the painting's life. The pictorial reinstatement was essentially conservative in character and carried out exclusively in watercolour, integrating by vertical or cross hatching only the lacunae and especially those caused by the sixteenth century cracks.

Special attention was devoted to the photographic and graphic documentation of the work. In the first case some 15,000 photographs between colour and black and white were taken relating to the stages before, during and after cleaning: a documentation which comprises, besides the standard shots with direct light, those with raking light, with ultraviolet and infra-red.

Since the mass of data emerging from the cleaning appeared impressive, in 1986 it was decided to turn to computers taking advantage of financial backing from Baron H. von Thyssen Bornemisza. A photogrammetric survey was carried out first of all, both on the ceiling and the Judgement on which it was planned to use the same methods, and by means of the relief basic information was acquired relating to the altimetric outline of the frescoed surface and the profile of the painted images. The acquisition of these elements and the digital development of the images that followed made it possible to work out the basic graphs on which to insert the data concerning the restoration, the state of preservation of the frescoes and the technique employed by Michelangelo to execute them. On the 23rd January 1987 the computer which is still employed today for archiving the aforementioned data was installed on the scaffolding. It is an Apollo DN 3000, with basic software

⇦
The figures of Christ the Judge and the Virgin Mary during the cleaning. On the lower part of Christ's raised arm is visible a correction by Michelangelo done "a secco" which changes the arm to a new position

Series 5000 and applied software provided by E.C.G. p.l.c., the company charged with carrying out the project. The applied software was afterwards improved by the restoration team in order to adapt it to the needs that emerged during the course of the work.

From the very beginning a strong need was felt to supplement the normal documentation with a film that would illustrate the cleaning as it progressed: chosen for this purpose was the Nippon Television Network from Tokyo which, starting from 1981 has faithfully filmed the phases of the cleaning taking some 45,000 metres of 16 mm. film in all.

Given the importance and the responsibility involved in the task undertaken and its absolute novelty, even more disturbing for those who had worked before than for others, it was understood from the very beginning that it was unthinkable to await the end of the operation to disclose the results achieved.

The Chapel therefore was constantly open to the public with the scaffolding set up in such a way as to cover only a small part of the frescoed surface, so as to allow everyone to follow the development of the cleaning. On the scaffolding there was regular access for a public restricted for practical and security reasons, to experts—art historians and restorers—who through their presence automatically ensured the most natural form of control of the operation under way.

Totally different was the scaffolding used for the restoration of the Judgement, just as the problems posed by this operation were very different. The Judgement could not be divided and cleaned section by section, like the ceiling where there existed an architectural frame and the cleaning therefore could not do without a deeply studied knowledge of the entire frescoed surface and preliminary tests carried out at every level of the painting. The scaffolding consequently hid the Judgement until the close of the operation and was equipped with 7 work platforms which make it possible to reach every point of the 180.2 sq.ms. of its surface.

Lunette with Eleazar; Mathan was the first figure to be cleaned
(on the top left, the figure before the cleaning)

The technique employed by Michelangelo denotes many differences as regards the ceiling, mainly connected with the use of lapis lazuli—a very delicate colour—for the blue of the sky, to the presence of some parts executed entirely *a secco* and finally in the use of some paints, such as vegetable lacquer and giallolino, which require the use of a binder.

Unlike the ceiling the Judgement also shows a great deal of retouching and repainting due mainly to its different logistic position and the ease with which it can be reached.

Among the repaintings, the so-called "braghe", painted in fresco for the figures of St. Blaise and St. Catherine and *a secco* in all other cases, have a very particular character.

Contrary to what is generally imagined, not all the "braghe" date back to the operation decided upon by the vote of the Council of Trent: many of them show a different fluorescence and it is possible that some may have been done even in fairly recent times.

Given the painting's technical characteristics and state of conservation, the cleaning method adopted on the Judgement is very different from that used for the ceiling. It

Lunette with Jacob; detail of Joseph after the cleaning
(on the facing page a detail before the cleaning)

consists of a preliminary washing with only distilled water and subsequent treatment with a solution of water and 25% ammonium carbonate, alternated with a phase using nitrate thinner.

After 24 hours the application of ammonium carbonate is repeated, applied through four sheets of Japanese paper. The treatment lasts about 9 minutes, after which the paper is removed and the part cleaned with a small sponge, soaked in the same ammonium carbonate solution. Further washings with distilled water follow. This method has given ex-

cellent results on the figures. Slightly different methods were employed for the sky, in the sense that the application of the ammonium carbonate solution lasts for a shorter time and, since the paint cannot be cleaned even with a very soft brush, the removal of extraneous substances is done with a pad: that is to say, a sponge soaked in water is placed on the painted surface and pressed against it in order to suck up the dirt contained in the pigment as it is released without causing friction.

The Chapel is now free of the conditions

which in the past caused the rapid deterioration of its frescoed decoration, but the problem of pollution remains in the long-term. For the future however the application of resinous or other substances, fatally destined to undergo change in the space of a few years, will no longer be used for the protection of the frescoes: on the basis of information obtained from the research carried out between 1983 and 1986 by V. Camuffo and A. Bernardi, a conditioning system with a monitored annual cycle which provides the filtering of the air entering the Chapel was realised instead, in such a way as to prevent the access of noxious gases and other polluting substances and to ensure ideal thermohygrometric conditions. The climatization system was provided by Delchi Carrier technology and includes continuous climatic monitoring with 75 sensors connected to a computer which automatically controls the atmospheric conditions inside the Sistine Chapel. The system was installed in July of 1992 with the collaboration of Vatican City Technical Services.

Other measures taken, or in the process of being taken, are the laying on the stairs leading to the Chapel of a special carpet for the purpose of retaining the dust brought in by visitors and the installation of a new lighting plant, a result of OSRAM technology, with

bulbs the positioning and power of which are such as to elude rising air currents thus guaranteeing optimal illumination of the paintings since the natural light coming from outside would be insufficient.

The restoration of the fifteenth century artists' work was carried out under the direction of D. Redig de Campos, by Igino Cupelloni assisted by G. Grossi, M. Rossi, M. De Luca, G. Properzi, G. Rossi de Gasteris. The operation under way for both the ceiling and the Judgement is being carried out by G. Colalucci with M. Rossi, P.G. Bonnetti, and B. Baratti; the work is being directed by F. Mancinelli; supervised by Carlo Pietrange-li, Director-General of the Museums; the techno-scientific consultancy up to 1991 was entrusted to P. Rotondi, who died recently, and after that date given to G. Torraca; analyses and laboratory research are conducted by N. Gabrielli assisted by F. Morresi, L. Gandini and G. Barnia; the photographic documentation of the restoration is being carried out by F. Bono, A. Bracchetti, D. Pivato, P. Zigrossi and the filmed part by N. T. V. of Tokyo; the archiving of the restoration documentation is under F. Petrignani; archive research is being conducted by A. M. De Strobel and, in the initial phase, by E. Cicerchia.

*Detail of an autograph by Michelan-
gelo with a sketch that shows a figure
painting the vault.
Florence, Buonarroti Archives*

The cleaning of the Last Judgement

*The moveable scaffold
constructed for the cleaning
of the frescoes on the vault*

Short History of the Sistine Chapel

1277-1280	Papacy of Nicholas III; the "*Palatium Novum*" (south and east wings of the Cortile del Pappagallo) is founded, including the *Capella Magna* which existed before the present-day Sistine Chapel.
c 1357	Papacy of Urban V: probable foundation of the *Capella Magna*.
1477	Renovation of the *Capella Magna* by Sixtus IV.
1480	Completion of the renovation work.
27-10-1481	Contract for ten frescoes in the Chapel awarded to Cosimo Rosselli, Botticelli, Ghirlandaio and Perugino.
c 1482	Signorelli is called to replace Ghirlandaio.
9-8-1483	Sixtus IV celebrates the anniversary of his election to the Papacy with a mass in the Sistine Chapel.
15-8-1483	Sixtus IV consecrates the Chapel to the Virgin of the Assumption.
1484-1492	Papacy of Innocent VIII (G. B. Cybo); the sacristy to the east of the Chapel is built.
May 1504	The *Capella* starts having stability problems.
10-5-1506	Letter from Pietro Rosselli to Michelangelo in which he mentions Julius II's intention of asking the artist to fresco the ceiling of the Chapel.
10-5-1508	The contract is signed and Michelangelo receives the first payment for his work in the Chapel. Beginning of the construction of the scaffolding to be used in the decoration of the ceiling.
Summer 1508/ 31-10-1512	Michelangelo frescoes the ceiling.
1-11-1512	Julius II "uncovered the ceiling on the morning of All Saints: the Pope went to the Chapel to celebrate mass with great satisfaction for the whole city" (Vasari).
1515	Leo X commissions from Raphael the cartoons for the tapestries to be hung in the Sistine Chapel.
1517-1519	The tapestries are woven in Bruxelles in the workshop of Pieter van Aelst.
26-12-1519	On the day after Christmas the tapestries are hung for the first time in the Chapel.
25-12-1522	The lintel of the entrance door in the Chapel collapses killing two of the Swiss guards of Hadrian VI's private corps.
1533	Clement VII (Giulio de' Medici) comissions Michelangelo to paint the Last Judgment on the wall behind the altar.
16-4-1535	Paul III reconfims this commission to Michelangelo. The scaffolding needed to paint the fresco is built.
1536	Michelangelo begins work.
31-10-1541	Paul III celebrates Vespers in front of the Last Judgment, which has just been uncovered.
21-1-1564	The Council of Trent issues the decree *Picturae in Capella Apostolica coperiantur*.
1565	Daniele da Volterra paints the first *braghe* ("underpants") on the Judgment.
1566-1585	Papacy of St. Pius V and Gregory XIII. Construction of the external buttresses of the Chapel. Domenico Carnevali retouches the Sacrifice of Noah. Matteo da Lecce and Hendrick van der Broeck repaint the damaged frescoes on the entrance wall.
1625	The Chapel is entirely cleaned by Simone Lagi on behalf of Pope Urban VIII.
1710-1712	Restoration of the Chapel by Annibale Mazzuoli for Pope Clement XI.
1762	Probable restoration by Stefano Pozzi who also covered the nudes in the Last Judgment.
28-6-1797	The explosion of the powder-magazine at Castel Sant'Angelo causes the colapse of the Ignudo to the left of the Delphic Sibyl and of a fragment of the Flood.
1825	Vincenzo Camuccini does some cleaning work on the Last Judgment.
1903-1904	Restoration of the ceiling and of the Last Judgment by Cingolani and Cecconi-Principi, under the supervision of Seitz.
1923-1924; 1936-1938	Continuation of restoration work on the ceiling by Biagetti.
1966-1974	Restoration of the fifteenth-century frescoes under the supervision of D. Redig de Campos.
1975	Restoration of the roof and the battlement.
1979-1980	Restoration of the frescoes on the entrance wall.
1980-1984	Restoration of the portraits of the Popes.
1980	The cleaning of Michelangelo's frescoes begins.
1989	Completion of the cleaning of the vault.
1990-1994	Cleaning of the Last Judgement.
1996-1999	Cleaning of the fifteenth-century frescoes.

Bibliography

The text regarding the 16th Century decoration of the Chapel is excerpted and updated from the writings of F. Mancinelli, *Michelangelo Pittore:* by F. MANCINELLI, R. BELLINI, *Michelangelo,* Editor Il Fiorino, Florence 1992.

CONDIVI Ascanio, *Vita di Michelangelo Buonarroti,* Rome 1553 (ed. Karl Frey, Berlin 1887).

VASARI Giorgio, *Le vite de' più eccellenti pittori scultori ed architetti,* Florence 1568 (ed. Milanesi, Florence 1885).

WÖLFFLIN Heinrich, *Ein Entwurf Michelangelos zur Sixtinischen Decke* in "Jahrbuch der Königlich Preußischen Kunstsammlungen" XIII, 1892, p. 178 ff.

KLACZKO Julian, *Jules II,* Paris 1898, 3rd ed. Paris 1902.

JUSTI Karl, *Michelangelo,* Leipzig 1900; 2nd ed. Berlin 1922.

STEINMANN Ernst, *Die Sixtinische Kapelle:* Vol. I, *Bau und Schmuck der Kapelle unter Sixtus IV,* Munich 1901; Vol. II, *Michelangelo,* Munich 1905.

THODE Henry, *Michelangelo und das Ende der Renaissance,* 6 vol., Berlin 1902-1913.

PANOFSKY Erwin, *Die Sixtinische Decke,* Leipzig 1921.

STEINMANN Ernst and WITTKOWER Rudolf, *Michelangelo-Biographie 1510-1926,* Leipzig 1927.

TOLNAY Charles de, *Michelangelo:* Vol. II, *The Sistine Ceiling,* Princeton 1945.

GUTMAN Harry B., *Religiöser Symbolismus in Michelangelos Sintflut-Fresko* in "Zeitschrift fur Kunstgeschichte" 18, 1955, p. 164 ff.

REDIG DE CAMPOS Deoclecio, *Drei Bedeutungen des Jüngsten Gerichts Michelangelos* in "Römische Quartalschrift" 59, 1964, p. 230 ff.

REDIG DE CAMPOS Deoclecio, *Il Giudizio Universale,* Milan 1964.

ISERMEYER Christian Adolf, *Literaturbericht - Das Michelangelo-Jahr 1964 und die Forschungen zu Michelangelo als Maler und Bildhauer von 1959-64,* in "Zeitschrift fur Kunstgeschichte" 28, 1965, p. 307 ff.

SALVINI Roberto, CAMESASCA Ettore, RAGGHIANTI Carlo Ludovico *La Cappella Sistina in Vaticano,* Milan 1965.

ETTLINGER Leopold David, *The Sistine Chapel before Michelangelo, Religious Imagery and Papal Primacy,* Oxford 1965.

CAMESASCA Ettore, *Michelangelo pittore,* Milan 1966.

REDIG DE CAMPOS Deoclecio, *I "tituli" degli affreschi del Quattrocento nella Cappella Sistina* in "Rendiconti della Ponteficia Accademia Romana di Archeologia", XLII 1969-1970, p. 299-314.

SHEARMAN J., *Raphael's Cartoons,* London 1972.

CHASTEL André, *Gli affreschi di Michelangelo nel Vaticano,* photographs by T. Okamura, Tokio 1980.

CHASTEL A., COLALUCCI G., DE VECCHI T., HIRST M., MANCINELLI F., O'MALLEY J., SHEARMAN J., *La Cappella Sistina. I primi restauri: la scoperta del colore,* Novara, New York, London, Barcelona, Tokio, Paris, Zurich, Tielf 1986.